# COLTISHALL

## HEYDA[illegible] [illegible]GE

### VICTORIAN BC[illegible]

"There is a great [illegible] age." So in 1881 declared William [illegible] s veteran Victorian schoolmaster. Headmaster of the village school for 32 years, he observed the rough and tumble of parish life in an age of profound social upheaval. Foul-mouthed youths waged gang warfare in the streets, vandalising property, insulting passers-by and terrorising the neighbourhood. Drunken men spilled from local public houses to brawl in the gutter. Yet this was Coltishall's "golden age" - a time when the village ranked among Norfolk's most dynamic and prosperous rural communities. Vigorous economic growth, highlighted by the development of a major malting industry and a celebrated wherrybuilding yard, earned Coltishall the description "town" in journals of the day.

Well-to-do Victorians admired the vitality of local life. They visited Coltishall Regatta, a spectacular water frolic of sailing boats and wherries which drew crowds to the riverside each autumn. They treated their children to the hoop-la stalls, coconut shies and merry-go-rounds of the annual Whit Monday fair on the Upper Common, taking care to avoid the mob which attended later in the day. They looked forward to the arrival of old-time touring circuses, when bands of musicians paraded village streets in open-topped waggons pulled by elephants. And they watched the North Norfolk Harriers stage annual stag hunts through the centre of the parish. The quarry was uncarted in the village and pursued by hounds and hunters into open countryside. Harper's pupils gave chase to the hunt in such numbers that he had little alternative but to declare a half-day holiday.

Coltishall had all the hustle and bustle of a large, lively community. Fleets of black-sailed trading wherries, stacked with coal and corn, berthed at village staithes each day. Noisy cattle markets were held once a week beside the railway station after the opening of the branch line in 1879. Nearly 200 children crowded into Harper's bulging school. Christians - Anglican, Methodist, Wesleyan and Salvationist - packed the churches. Nine pubs did a roaring trade quenching the thirst of a rapidly-growing population. Coltishall's horse-drawn fire brigade, manned by volunteers, did its best to cope with blaze dramas. An abundance of craftsmen, including blacksmiths (four in 1881 alone), tailors, shoemakers, thatchers, basketmakers, harnessmakers, wheelwrights, malt shovel makers, jewellers and watchmakers, made the village a hive of activity. There was also a cottage hospital, a bank and a reading room.

Coltishall rose to its Victorian heyday thanks to a series of key economic advantages. They included a navigable river, placing the village on the busy Aylsham-Yarmouth trade route; a productive agriculture, enclosed since the sixteenth century and efficiently cultivated under the Norfolk four-course system; valuable natural resources, including mature woodlands, first-class soil, marl, chalk, clay and sand; a position on the Norwich-North Walsham coaching route; proximity to the emerging Broads tourist industry; extensive limeworks; a brick-making yard; a brewing industry; a wealth of shops; a skilled, industrious workforce led by men of enterprise and vision, and a rising population of mainly young people. Before the First World War Coltishall enjoyed a pre-eminence within its immediate locality of 15-20 parishes. It was a position which was subsequently lost following a change in the structure of the rural economy. Today there are few reminders of the Victorian boom town which emerged from the village's 2000-year-old history.

## ROMAN ORIGINS

Coltishall has Roman roots. The village was a key point on the Roman navigation linking Burgh-next-Aylsham and Burgh Castle. Roman bricks and tiles, presumably taken from derelict local buildings, were used in the rebuilding of the parish church in the thirteenth century. Several Roman urns were unearthed in 1810 in a marlpit beside the North Walsham Road, and more urns, with coins and vases, came to light in 1850. Further evidence of Roman occupation was uncovered during the Second World War when deep ploughing, in the area subsequently developed as Church Close, revealed the foundations of a Roman settlement. Roman coins dating from the late third or early fourth centuries were found in two Church Close gardens in 1965 and 1973.

The invasion of England in the fifth and sixth centuries by the Saxon people of northern Germany further shaped the formation of the village. Due to Coltishall's position as a crossing point on the Bure settlement again took place, and parish lands were brought under regular cultivation. The Saxons built a place of worship on the site of the present parish church. Two small circular Saxon windows, incorporated into the north wall of the church during the thirteenth century, can still be seen today. The name Coltishall, according to eighteenth century Norfolk historian Francis Blomefield, derives from a Saxon owner. The Anglo-Saxon family names Coc and Coker have both been linked with the village, which appeared as Cokereshala and Coketeshala in the Domesday Book. The village was later known as Cowteshale, Coltsale, Coultsale, Couteshall and Coulteshall before settling down to its present-day spelling in the seventeenth century.

By the time of the Norman Conquest Coltishall was an established parish under the jurisdiction of the Crown, with a population of some 150. The Domesday survey, completed in 1086, records that William de Warren was Lord of the Manor and that 110 acres of land were held by the Turold family. The church was endowed with 10 acres of glebe land and the village had five plough teams, confirming the view that the locality was under systematic cultivation. The manor had by the thirteenth century passed to the Hackford family and was later held by the Seckford family and Duchy of Lancaster.

Coltishall people were given special privileges in an extraordinary charter authorised in 1231 by Henry III. It granted "to all men, women and children born, or to be born, in this village of Couteshall, freedom from all

Coltishall Lower Common earlier this century. Note the malthouse to the left of the Rising Sun and the old Salvation Army hall in front of the King's Head. (W.Rout)

villenage of body and blood; and from toll, stallage, picage and pannage, in all fairs and markets throughout England." It added that "all frays, transgressions, bargains, quarrels and suits concerning the said town of Couteshall, should be determined twice every year, before the King's officers at the leets (manorial courts) there." The charter effectively released villagers from the bonds of serfdom, making them freemen at a time when the vast majority of ordinary people lived under the total control of feudal lords. Blomefield regarded the charter as a great honour for Coltishall, but was at a loss to explain why the village should have been singled out for such special attention. In 1425 Henry VI conveyed all his rights over Coltishall to King's College, Cambridge, who remain Lords of the Manor today.

The thirteenth century was notable for the establishment of Great

Hautbois Hospital close to the now-ruined St. Theobald Church. A religious house, the hospital was founded at the head of an ancient causeway to care for travellers and local poor. A castle is said to have been built at or near the site of the hospital in 1312. Both institutions had fallen into ruin by the sixteenth century. Chalk and marl digging increased river trade in the middle ages and by the seventeenth century vessels were bringing coal and various other commodities to Coltishall from Yarmouth, returning with cargoes of corn, timber, chalk, marl, local-brewed beer and, probably, malt. Contemporary prosperity brought the village a number of fine buildings, including Coltishall Hall, The Limes and several Queen Anne houses with distinctive gable ends. The completion of the Aylsham Navigation in the late eighteenth century, which allowed wherries to sail as far as Aylsham Mill, helped launch Coltishall into a period of sustained economic growth with the coming of the industrial age.

## MALTING CENTRE

Malt was the making of Victorian Coltishall. A thriving malting industry sprang up in the village in the years following the industrial revolution. By the 1880s malting was the cornerstone of the local economy, employing more than 100 men in some 18 malthouses along the banks of the Bure. As many as 20 wherries, fully laden with first-class brewing malt, sailed from the village each day. Thousands of tons of Coltishall malt were sold to breweries at home and abroad each year. Some was even made into Guinness. At the height of the brewing boom gangs of broad-shouldered maltsters worked

A view of the river looking towards Anchor Street at the beginning of this century. One of Anchor Street's large malthouses can be seen to the left of the Anchor Inn. (Mrs.M.Morse)

Untouched by the passing of time, the remains of a 200-year-old brewery are still to be found in an outbuilding at The Limes. Here Billy Stibbons, who has lived in the house since childhood, stands next to a mechanism used to grind malt in preparation for brewing. It was probably in use in Mary Hardy's day in the late 18th century. Picture by Brian Waite.

round the clock to cope with demand. Their back-breaking labours sent the aroma of roasted barley wafting through riverside streets for most of the year.

Malting at Coltishall had modest beginnings. The earliest malthouses, believed to have been built in the seventeenth century, supplied small parish breweries. Mary Hardy's eighteenth century diary refers to the busy malthouse at The Limes, where Coltishall "nog" (strong ale) was brewed by the barrel load in an adjacent brew-house, part of which survives today. A succession of brewers, including Chapman and George Ives, Siday and Robert Hawes, Davy Postle and Samuel Buck, continued the village brewing tradition into the 1860s.

The nineteenth century witnessed an unprecedented growth in demand for malt from newly-developed urban breweries all over Britain. This, coupled with the development of efficient river transport, created the conditions in which Coltishall's malting industry was able to flourish. Parish farmland grew top quality malting barley, and sulphate of lime and hard water, both important in the malting process, were abundant local resources. Specialist companies, including Mealing and Mills, built modern malthouses at various locations in the village between 1800-50. One of these, described

Men of malt. Coltishall maltsters face the camera in the period 1850-75 *(above)* and about 1914 *(below)*. Both pictures were taken at the same malthouse in Anchor Street beside the Anchor Inn. (W.Rout)

as "most substantial and recently erected," was sold at a Norwich auction in 1842. "The malthouse is in a fine barley district, is equipped with the best and latest improvements, and stands unrivalled for the shipment of malt through Yarmouth to the Metropolis," said a sale notice. By the 1850s extensive malting complexes were to be found near the Rising Sun, King's Head and London Tavern, at the Manor House, Limes, White House, Holly Lodge and Old House, beside the river bridge and along Anchor Street and White Lion Road. In the space of 50 years the Victorian working man's taste for beer had made malting Coltishall's staple industry.

A seasonal occupation, malting took place between about September and May. Within those months gangs of maltsters, working inside cramped, stuffy malthouses, converted sacks of barley into malt. To do so they forced the germination of the grain by soaking - or "steeping" - it in water for about three days and spreading it in thick layers across wide tiled floors. The grain was regularly turned with rakes, forks and shovels, and in the warmth of the malthouse green shoots would start to appear. As soon as germination had occurred, the barley was dried and roasted over a coal-fired kiln. Burnt shoots were then removed in a process known as "jamming the kiln, "when men and boys tramped over the grain wearing rope-soled boots. Finally, the malt was bagged up and loaded on to wherries at nearby staithes. Coltishall malthouses, which were built on two floors, maintained continuous production during winter months. No sooner had one laden wherry set sail for Yarmouth than another was waiting to be loaded. During the summer the maltsters helped with the harvest, skippered pleasure wherries for Broads holidaymakers and worked in local boatyards.

Maltsters formed a large working-class community at the heart of village life. They were rough, tough men who worked hard and played hard. Each maltster was expected to carry 16-stone sacks of barley as part of his daily duties. After a day of heavy lifting some returned home with shoulders covered with blood. Small wonder that malting has been described as the hardest work next to coal mining. It was also hot and thirsty. Maltsters toiled for long periods close to kilns which were kept at a constant 220 degrees Fahrenheit. To prevent dehydration the men drank large quantities of beer before going to work. Eight or nine pints before breakfast was quite normal when malting started at dawn. Every drop was sweated off by the end of the day. Malting was skilled work which, by the standards of the day, was well paid. A maltster earned about half as much again as a farm worker.

Malting gangs were instantly recognisable in their grubby workclothes and distinctive red tassled hats. They worked as highly-disciplined teams and were bound together by a strong spirit of camaraderie. Individuals were known by colourful nicknames - "Spot" Tunmore, "Trip" Clements and "Preacher" Evans among them. When work finished for the day they crowded into village pubs to drink prodigious amounts of ale. It was said that

Coltishall maltsters had "two-gallon guts," such was their drinking capacity. The rowdy behaviour of drunken maltsters, who often brawled in the street late at night, was of great concern to more sober and upstanding members of the community, most notably the schoolmaster, William Harper. Maltsters were among the first converts of the Salvation Army, which sought to stamp out drunkenness and ruffianism by holding open-air meetings beside the Rising Sun and King's Head a century ago. Sixteen wayward souls were "saved" at the first service in 1885, conducted by three Salvationists who marched all the way from Norwich for the occasion.

Five wherries ready to be loaded at the malthouse staithe beside the Rising Sun, c.1914. Walter Rout, who lent the author this picture, is the boy standing at the tiller of the wherry in the foreground.

Malting at Coltishall reached its zenith before the turn of the century. Local malt was shipped to Ireland, the Netherlands and numerous domestic breweries in the final years of the Victorian era. After a period of rationalisation in the 1880s, when smaller malthouses, including those at the Manor House, were allowed to close, production was concentrated at the larger complexes of Anchor Street, White Lion Road and in the vicinity of the Rising Sun and London Tavern. The branch railway was also used to quicken the transportation of malt. In the late nineteenth century R.S. Watling and

Son, the Yarmouth-based malting firm, took over the leases of Coltishall's malthouses in a move which revitalised the industry. Watlings embarked on a modernisation programme and won a lucrative contract to supply the giant breweries of Guinness. The contract secured the future of the industry into the Edwardian era. After the First World War, however, local malthouses were exposed as uneconomic. Unmechanised, labour intensive and isolated from the main centres of demand, they fell victim to the larger malting plants which had been built beside mainline railways in other parts of the country. The last remaining Coltishall malthouses were shut down in the winter of

A laden wherry passes through Coltishall lock at the turn of the century. On the left is the now-ruined lock-keeper's house. (Norfolk Museums Service)

1926-27, following the end of the Guinness contract. Some older villagers believe there was a labour dispute over wages before the closure. Young redundant maltsters left the village in search of work at maltings at Burton-on-Trent and Stowmarket. Others found local employment in boatyards and on farms.

The loss of the malting industry, and the vigorous working community it supported, was a major blow to Coltishall's status as a centre of rural prosperity. Malting was the lynchpin of the entire village economy. It consumed as much barley as local farmers could grow. It helped generate the booming wherry-borne river trade which sustained the Anchor Street boatbuilding yard. It gave endless work to village craftsmen, from malt shovel makers to blacksmiths, carpenters to bricklayers. And, not least, it employed a group of workers whose sheer spending power breathed life into shops and pubs. Closure of the malthouses precipitated the break-up of Coltishall's traditional economy and can therefore be seen as an important watershed in the history of the parish. Not since the days of malting has so large an occupational community of local-born people lived and worked in the village. Since their closure the malthouses have been demolished, converted to residential use or made into greenhouses and garden stores. One has been used as a swimming pool; another as a granary. The former maltings next to the bridge is today an abattoir.

## BIRTHPLACE OF THE WHERRY

Long before Anchor Street became the fashionable, affluent neighbourhood it is today, a collection of ramshackle boatsheds stood on the banks of the Bure. Tucked away behind the old Anchor Inn, they were the workplace of Coltishall's wherrybuilders, a tough breed of craftsmen renowned throughout Broadland for their boatbuilding skills. Their daily labours filled the riverside air with the smell of pitch pine, varnish, linseed oil, oak chips, tar, paint and burning rushes. In more than a century of wherrybuilding they turned out some 80 majestic black-sailed traders, which graced local waterways from the dawn of the industrial age to the Second World War.

Reputed to be the birthplace of the Norfolk wherry, Coltishall was probably the oldest boatbuilding centre on the Broads. Norfolk keels - forerunners of the wherry - are believed to have been constructed at Anchor Street, so it is conceivable that the boatyard there dated from the sixteenth century, or even earlier. Firm evidence of the yard's existence comes rather later, however. Its first mention in parish records is in 1823, when Thomas Wright occupied the site. Demolition of an old boatshed in 1836 revealed the date 1801 inscribed on a beam. Coltishall diarist Mary Hardy, writing in 1776, recorded the building of a wherry for her husband William, a local farmer and brewer.

Whatever the origins of the Anchor Street boatyard, its emergence as a major wherrybuilding centre can clearly be traced from 1864. It was in October of that year that John Allen bought the yard for £400 at an auction at the White Horse Inn, Coltishall. With shrewd, skilful stewardship he took the yard to the height of its prosperity, employing a team of the finest craftsmen in Norfolk. From the 1860s to the turn of the century an average of one new wherry each year was launched into the Bure at Coltishall. Of all Broadland's boatyards, only Halls of Reedham built more.

Allen's men constructed the fastest wherries in Norfolk. Built for the narrow waters of the Ant and Bure, they were long, slender and comparatively light. The 20-ton 'Cornucopia', for example, launched at Coltishall in 1893, weighed about half as much as wherries built elsewhere. The 'Ella', completed in 1912, was said to be the smallest and fastest wherry ever built. Tailor-made for the North Walsham-Dilham canal, she was just 11 feet wide. Another Coltishall wherry, the 22-ton 'Helen', was a famous prize-winner in races on Wroxham Broad in the 1880s and 1890s. The names of several other Coltishall wherries were carved on the rafters of an Anchor Street boatshed, pulled down in the 1930s. Among them were the 60-foot 'Orion' (later re-named 'Gleaner'), launched in 1894, 'Primus' (1896), 'Emily' (1897), 'Hilda' (1898), 'Dispatch' (1900) and 'Secunda' (1902). Each plied local rivers

Aristocrats of labour. Coltishall boatbuilders gather for a photograph in the late 19th century, probably at the launching of a new wherry. The boatyard owner, John Allen, is second from the left, seated. (Norfolk County Libraries)

for many years with cargoes of malt, timber, grain, marl, reeds, sand and coal.

The boatbuilders of Anchor Street were aristocrats of labour who commanded considerable status in village life. They served strict seven-year apprenticeships to learn the skills of the trade, and were obliged to forego numerous personal freedoms. Robert Collins, later a well-known Wroxham wherrybuilder, was articled as a 14-year-old to Coltishall boatbuilder Samuel Press in 1863. Under the terms of his apprenticeship he was

A steam traction engine hauls newly-felled oak trees to the sawpit of Allens boatyard at the turn of the century. Timber from the trees was used to make wherries. (A.Lewis)

The Coltishall-built wherry 'Cornucopia' at Barton Regatta in 1929. (Norfolk County Libraries)

forbidden for seven years from marrying, fornicating, playing cards or dice and visiting what were described as "playhouses." And for the privilege of this apprenticeship, his father had to pay Press a fee of £15 - a substantial sum in those days.

Working from dawn till dusk in an organised chaos of crumbling workshops, lean-to paint sheds and rat-ridden wood piles, the village boatbuilders were a unique occupational community. They built and repaired wherries with near religious devotion, jealously guarding the reputation of their yard. Each wherry was built without plans or drawings. Huge oak trees were felled from local estates and hauled to the boatyard sawpit, where they were cut and later transformed into superb clinker-built craft. Every part of the wherry, from tabernacle to tiller, stem to slipping keel, was hand-made. Sails and rigging were brought from Yarmouth and metal work was completed by a village blacksmith. The boatyard artisans frequently gathered at the Anchor Inn at the end of a hard day's work.

The march of progress brought an end to wherrybuilding at Coltishall. Railways and motorised road transport took cargo away from the waterways. Old riverside industries such as malting, which had provided the wherries

Clifford Allen, the last in a long line of wherrybuilders, at the helm of the wherry 'Solace' at Coltishall in 1973. (Courtesy Eastern Daily Press)

Allens boatyard - complete with a newly-built wherry - shortly after the turn of the century. The Anchor Inn can be seen in the background. (Norfolk Heritage)

with much of their cargo, were forced to close as larger, more efficient plants were built elsewhere. Demand for new wherries finally collapsed in the Edwardian era. The last trading wherry ever to be built in Norfolk, the 'Ella', was launched at Coltishall in 1912. In the face of the decline of the wherry, Coltishall boatyard started to produce new craft. As early as 1888 Allen's craftsmen were turning out sailing yachts for leisure use. Wherry yachts, such as the 'White Rose', were launched from the 1890s. After the First World War the yard kept busy by maintaining the scores of wherries which continued to work on local rivers. The yard also built and hired out numerous Broads cruisers. Business continued until 1974, when Clifford Allen - the fourth generation of his family to run the yard - sold the site. Boatyard buildings were unceremoniously demolished to make way for Boatyard Maltings, a modern residential development.

None of the Coltishall wherries are still afloat. Each was laid to rest on a river bed as soon as its useful life was over. Their rotting remains are still to be seen scattered around the Broadland landscape. The 'Ella', the last to be consigned to a watery grave, was sunk in a dyke at the entrance to Decoy Broad in the 1960s. She needed £2000 worth of repairs, but nobody wanted to restore her. Today, she lies forgotten, ripped apart by the ravages of more than 20 years of frost, wind and rain. Like all her kind, she is beyond saving. It is a tragedy that none of the Coltishall wherries was preserved as a tribute to the craftsmanship of Anchor Street's bygone boatbuilders.

# "A BAD NEIGHBOURHOOD"

William Harper, a kind and dedicated schoolmaster, was probably the most hated man in Victorian Coltishall. In 32 years as headmaster of the village school he was kicked, insulted, threatened with prosecution and assaulted with a knife. Local parents waged an undeclared war against Harper from the moment he set foot in Coltishall in 1874, resorting to tactics of violence and intimidation to disrupt school life. Resistance reached a peak in the summer of 1889, when three mothers from St.James attempted to force his dismissal by making baseless allegations that he had beaten their children. Harper survived the crisis, and lived to tell a remarkable story about the kind of village Coltishall was a century ago.

Wiltshire-born Harper was the first schoolmaster of Coltishall Board School. His appointment followed the passing of the Education Act in 1870, which introduced elementary education for all. With the help of his wife, Elizabeth, a schoolmistress, his task was to teach a largely illiterate village to read and write. But it was not that simple. The Act provoked bitter opposition in poverty-stricken Norfolk, where children were put to work by their parents to make ends meet. Coltishall was no exception. "Many parents in this benighted spot speak of the Education Act as a tyrannous law", wrote Harper. "Like ignorant people generally they detest and fear what they do not understand. Children are taught at home to consider their teachers as gaolers and school as a prison."

Hostility to Harper's school took a variety of forms. Parents threw homework books on the fire. More commonly, they kept their children away from school altogether. Up to 70 per cent of Harper's pupils failed to turn up for long periods of the year. Some never attended. They were sent to work in the fields, scaring crows, picking stones, leading farm horses at drill, gathering turnips and helping with haymaking and harvesting. In the spring scores of children were employed peeling osiers, lengths of willow used for basket-making. After the start of the malting season youngsters were engaged "picking kiln", or clearing shoots of barley from the flagstones of village malthouses. In the autumn more than 100 scholars skipped off into local woods to gather bags of acorns, which they sold to farmers as winter pig feed. Sons of wherrymen disappeared with their fathers for months on end on voyages to Yarmouth and Norwich. "Compulsory attendance at school does not extend to Coltishall," wrote Harper. "Whenever a farmer wants a boy he takes him, notwithstanding Education Acts and by-laws."

Alarmed by the scale of truancy, Harper urged school authorities to take action to enforce attendance. This placed school governors in an awkward position, as some of them, including St. James farmer Charles Hood, employed children themselves. But by 1879 an attendance officer was employed to hunt out truants and drive them to school in a pony and trap.

More draconian measures followed. The school board, chaired by Norfolk magistrate Robert Gorell, started to issue court summonses against the parents of children who were persistently absent. Coltishall parents were hauled before magistrates at Aylsham on several occasions in the late nineteenth century. Fines of a few shillings were handed down.

The "get tough" approach towards compulsory attendance unleashed a tide of ill-will against Harper and his school. Hard-up local parents, struggling to bring up large families on 10 or 12 shillings a week, did not take kindly to being humiliated in court for putting their children to work. Reaction was swift. Parents started to instruct their offspring to disobey Harper in school. This was done, the schoolmaster noted in 1880, "in the hope that it will provoke corporal punishment, and the slightest touch will be blown up into a violent assault, and a spirit of rebellion will well up against the school board management."

A minority of pupils took their parents' call to revolution seriously. Without fear of punishment at home, a number of older boys began to defy Harper's every word, making his life hell for the next 20 years. If told to behave, they swore at him. If punished, they kicked and scratched him until, on at least one occasion, his legs and hands were covered with blood. Uncontrollable boys were locked away in the playground toilet. One such ruffian, confined in 1892, "made a disturbance in the lavatory," said Harper. "He was so violent the master (himself) had to tie his legs as he kicked about and defied him. He then got a knife and opened it, apparently with the intention of stabbing the master, but his hand was seized and the knife fortunately taken from him. Just then his mother came, swore at the teachers and took away her son."

Revengeful parents threatened Harper with summonses for assault if he laid a finger on their rebellious children. One boy, bracing himself for a caning in 1889, bellowed: "You'll get in a row if you touch me. I'll tell my mother. She'll have you summoned!" Harper suffered constant humiliation at the hands of parents. An irate father marched into school in 1893 to tell him in front of a full class that he was a disgrace to Coltishall. He also threatened to wring his nose. "Teachers have more trouble with the parents than with the children," reflected Harper. "This is a bad neighbourhood. It is surprising that so many of the children are so well behaved when one considers their surroundings and hears the language that the poor children are accustomed to at home."

The child-beating conspiracy of 1889 was the most malicious example of the parents' hate campaign against Harper. Three mothers, fearing prosecution by the school board because of their children's irregular attendance, got together and accused Harper, his wife and another teacher of beating their offspring. In fact, stated Harper, none of the children had been touched, and one of the mothers had severely beaten her son herself

Coltishall Board School at the turn of the century. The person standing in the doorway is believed to be William Harper.(Norfolk County Libraries)

the evening before to make her complaint appear more plausible. "The teachers believe it is a conspiracy to injure them," wrote Harper. The parents' plot failed.

Harper was acutely aware of the poverty in which many of his pupils lived. He noted that some families of nine or ten children were supported on 11 or 12 shillings a week. "It is a great temptation to parents to have four shillings a week offered for the services of a boy of 11 or 12." He was also concerned at the squalor of the Victorian age. He sent some pupils home because their clothes and hair were swarming with vermin. Epidemics spread like wildfire through the village. Scarlet fever, diptheria, influenza, chicken pox, mumps, whooping cough and measles all took their toll, closing the school for months on end. In the school year 1886-87 nine of Harper's pupils died of scarlet fever, measles and whooping cough. "Fever panic" swept through the village during the scarlet fever epidemic of that year, and Harper described how the tolling of the parish church bell at the funeral of two of the pupils frightened parents into keeping their children away from school until the epidemic had passed.

Harper despaired at the rowdyism of village life, and constantly referred to the "idle, rude street habits" of his pupils. He kept a close eye on the gangs of "up-town" and "down-town" boys who engaged in pitched battles along Church Street, fighting with sticks, throwing stones, vandalising property and striking boys who did not belong to their number. The "up-towners" were from the village west of the church, including High Street, and the "down-towners" from the east, including St.James and Anchor Street. In 1886 the ruffians disrupted a confirmation service at the church by making noises in the graveyard. Two years later Harper observed that several children had been hurt by the antics of the bully boys. A gang of pupils burgled and vandalised the school in 1903. Harper was also appalled at the behaviour of Coltishall's adult population. In 1895 he wrote: "After being closed for four days on account of the East Norfolk election, we resumed work yesterday and found that the disorderly scenes in the streets had produced a bad effect on some of the scholars. Seeing their big brothers, and in some cases their parents, in such an excited state, and hearing so much hooting and bad language addressed to people of opposite opinions to their own, some of the children were very impatient of discipline, and taxed the teachers' efforts to suppress their tendency to imitate the rowdy conduct they had witnessed in the streets."

In his brighter moments Harper looked forward to the day when parents would actually encourage their children to learn at school. "By that time the present teachers will have grown too old for work, or have been worried out of this life," he reflected. After a teaching career spanning 51 years, Harper retired in 1906. His retirement gift - an arm chair - was well earned. He moved from the old schoolhouse on the corner of Rectory Road to the Lower House, White Lion Road, where he lived until his death, aged 77, in 1918.

## OPEN ALL HOURS

"What you goin' to be in bed all day?" Victorian landlords of the London Tavern were woken by this impatient, familiar cry at 6 o'clock in the morning. Outside in the street, the story goes, gangs of thirsty maltsters hammered on the door, demanding their first pints of the day. It was time to open up.

Nine pubs, unlimited opening hours and plenty of strong, cheap ale made Coltishall a beer-drinker's dream 100 years ago. The village was full of working people with a taste for a tipple: wherrymen, farm labourers, boatbuilders, blacksmiths, the list is endless. Their late-night drinking exploits led all too often to fearsome street fighting, particularly between members of families locked in bitter, age-old feuds (and there were many of them). Violence also followed heavy day time drinking. The Whit Monday fair on the Upper Common invariably ended in a drunken brawl, with stalls overturned, benches scattered and fists flying. Villagers born around the turn of the century have vivid childhood memories of gathering beside the common to watch the fracas with their friends.

The Victorian licensed trade was so buoyant that a new tavern - appropriately called the New Inn - was built by Morgans brewery in the first half of the century. Later renamed the Railway, it joined the Cabinet Maker's Arms, White Horse, London Tavern, Red Lion, King's Head, Rising Sun, White Lion and Anchor.

In Mary Hardy's day, in the 1770s, harvest frolics were held at the White Horse. The pub boasted a fine bowling green and later became known as Coltishall's principal inn. In the 1880s village schoolmaster William Harper complained that some of his boys were picking up bad habits by wiping bowls at the White Horse to earn pocket money. In the late nineteenth century the pub landlady, Mary Press, advertised "well-aired beds, good stabling and lock-up coach houses."

Henry Child, publican of the London Tavern a century ago, ran a bakery behind the pub to supplement his income. So did his son and successor, Frederick. Local housewives took their pigs' fry to be cooked there. Children were sent on errands to buy "dumpling dough" from the bakehouse for their fathers' dinners. Elsewhere in Coltishall it was quite common for landlords to have second jobs. James Grout, the father-of-seven who kept the Red Lion in the 1880s, doubled as a maltster. So did Isaac Wright of the Rising Sun, who also traded in corn, cattle cake, coal and cinders from his staithe. White Lion publican George Ives was a brewer and butcher.

Coltishall has lost four of its nine Victorian pubs. The ancient White Lion, which stood on the site of White Lion Cottages in White Lion Road, closed towards the end of the last century. The Cabinet Maker's Arms, opposite the war memorial, served its last pint in the late 1950s, and the White Horse, beside the river bridge, shut in the early 1970s. The once-flourishing Anchor called time in 1985.

London Tavern landlord Frederick "Doughy" Child (left) stands outside his pub, c.1904. A passage leading to his bakery is on the left of the picture. (W.Stibbons)

# THE DAY THE RAINS CAME...

A freak deluge brought Coltishall to a standstill in the summer of 1912. More than seven inches of rain fell on the village in a ferocious downpour lasting two days. After the worst of the storm had passed, Coltishall - and much of Horstead, too - was engulfed by a surge of water so vast that it swept away the river bridge. A lone traveller from Swanton Abbott just managed to pass over the bridge on his horse and cart before it collapsed. The Bure burst its banks, sending a torrent of floodwater rushing through a bedraggled and bewildered parish. Streets turned into streams, houses crumbled and gardens subsided. Part of the White Horse Inn was washed away. Cottages made from marl lump dissolved, making some families homeless. The worst affected areas were High Street, White Lion Road, St. James and Anchor Street, where houses were filled with several feet of muddy water.

The cause of the trouble was Buxton Lock, which broke under the sheer weight of water. Three miles downstream, Coltishall got a real soaking. Local people took to the streets in rowing boats to help stranded neighbours. One of those rescued was four-year-old Billy Stibbons, whose family lived in White Lion Road at the time of the flood. His first memory is of being lowered into a rowing boat from an upstairs window. Sight-seers came from surrounding villages to survey the damage to Coltishall bridge. A ferry service was set up across the water. Rebuilding work was started almost immediately, and the present Coltishall bridge was completed in 1913. Havoc was caused throughout Norfolk by the legendary 1912 storm, which raged from August 26th-28th. Previous rainfall records were doubled. Crops were lost, livestock perished and railway services ground to a halt. Two people were drowned in Norwich.

"The Bure burst its banks, sending a torrent of floodwater rushing through a bedraggled and bewildered parish." Villagers gather on the Coltishall side of the ruined bridge during the 1912 flood. (E.Bush)

***Above:*** Coltishall's ancient bridge was destroyed in the Great Flood of 1912. (Norfolk County Libraries) ***Left:*** Workmen rebuilding the bridge in the winter of 1912-13. Sixth from the left is Bob Riseborough, whose daughter-in-law, Audrey Riseborough, kindly lent the author this rare photograph. ***Below:*** Coltishall's brand new bridge opened in 1913. (E.Bush)

The White Horse public house after the 1912 flood. As well as the ruined furniture, the walls are propped and there is a visible high water mark. (Norfolk County Libraries)

## GENIAL VICTORIAN RECTOR

Clergyman, farmer, lime-merchant, politician, educationalist, philanthropist, sportsman and wit - this was John Colk Girling, Coltishall's genial Victorian rector.

A chirpy and warm-hearted evangelist, Girling was one of the best-known parsons in Norfolk. Tales of his exploits were told throughout the diocese. An incurable gossip, it was said that he took three hours to walk across his parish, such was his love of pausing at street corners for a "mardle." Beneath a gregarious and slightly eccentric exterior, Girling was a shrewd businessman and an enlightened parish priest. He was constantly dreaming up ideas to benefit the village. Most were put into practice.

Girling was born at Paston in 1830, the younger son of a farmer. Educated at the Paston School, North Walsham, and Caius College, Cambridge, he served a brief curacy at Cromer before being ordained priest at Norwich Cathedral in 1857. He was appointed rector of Great Hautbois in 1859, and in 1880 succeeded the Rev. Joseph Thackeray as rector of Coltishall in addition to Hautbois.

On arrival at Hautbois, Girling was a wealthy young man of 28. Marriage in 1852 to Frances Wright, the daughter of a silk manufacturer and Norwich Union director, had made sure of that. Girling built himself a fine flint-faced rectory overlooking the river at Hautbois and, after holding a public meeting, decided to build a new church on its doorstep to replace the ancient parish church of St. Theobald. The present Hautbois church of Holy Trinity, consecrated in 1864, cost him more than £1000 - a fortune in Victorian times.

On weekdays Girling swapped his dog collar for a farmer's smock. Farming was his great love, and he cultivated a large acreage of glebe land at Hautbois. His pride and joy was a pedigree herd of Jerseys, and his

Genial rector - John Colk Girling MA. (Miss D.Girling)

reputation for farming prowess was known throughout the district. It was said that on Saturdays he preferred to go to market rather than write his sermons. He was also a keen sportsman, boasting a powerful - if portly - build. As a young man he was addicted to field sports and was known as a first-class shot. He was an enthusiastic huntsman and an accomplished Broads yachtsman.

Girling had not been long at Hautbois before he discovered a rich seam of marl in a meadow within a stone's throw of his rectory. Always with an eye for a business opportunity, he built three massive lime kilns on the meadow and started to employ gangs of labourers to dig the valuable clay soil

Dorothy Girling stands beside Holy Trinity Church, Great Hautbois, built by her grandfather, the Rev.John Colk Girling. Picture by Brian Waite.

from the ground. When roasted in the kilns the marl turned to lime, a sought-after agricultural fertiliser. The lime was taken to market by river, and Girling had a 100-yard cutting dug from the Bure towards the marl pit, creating a convenient loading point for wherries. Between the 1860s-90s Girling's workmen disgorged tens of thousands of tons of marl from the Hautbois pits, carving a giant excavation deep into the ground.

Fortunately for his parishioners, Girling had a social conscience. His wealth and privileges did not blind him to the appalling conditions in which many ordinary people lived, particularly during periods of unemployment. As one of the guardians of Aylsham Workhouse he was familiar with the harsh workings of the Victorian poor law, which divided families and caused untold misery. Girling called regularly at the homes of the poor in his parishes, offering help wherever he could. For example, he employed out-of-work labourers at his Hautbois lime pit.

Girling took positive steps to spread literacy among his parishioners. He set up a voluntary school in a coach house at his rectory and paid a schoolmaster to teach village children to read and write. He became a member of Coltishall School Board when it was formed in 1874, serving for some 30 years as chairman and vice-chairman. He enlivened community life by organising parish concerts and paying for seaside excursions for Sunday School pupils and his two church choirs. After the railway branch line opened in 1879 he hired train carriages for annual "treats" to Yarmouth, Mundesley, Cromer, Palling and Bacton.

His passion for politics knew no bounds. A zealous Conservative, he was a friend of Sir Edward Birkbeck, Tory M.P. for East Norfolk, who lived at Horstead Hall. At election time he joined Birkbeck's campaign trail, and was well-known for his rousing speeches from Conservative platforms across the constituency. In the run-up to the 1906 general election, Girling - then 76 years old - made a rollicking speech at a political meeting at the White Horse Inn at Coltishall, attacking the Liberal candidate. He promised the audience that in the event of a Tory victory he would preach from the pulpit "without money and without price." Happily for him, the Liberals won.

Girling was the father of 13 children, of whom only seven, including four sons, survived childhood. His wife was a withdrawn, aloof woman whose character was quite unlike that of her husband. She left the care of her brood to servants and spent most of her time in bed complaining of nerves. She lived to be 98.

An amiable, well-liked fellow, Girling had the knack of making friends with all sorts of people, including political opponents and dissenting churchmen. He took pleasure in telling anecdotes of old-time country life, and shared a dry sense of humour with Joseph Thackeray, rector of Coltishall and Horstead before 1880. Thackeray lived at Horstead Rectory, a house overlooked by Girling's newly-built Hautbois Rectory. One day Girling met his neighbour and boomed: "I look down on you, Thackeray!" "I turn my back on you, Girling!" came the retort.

Girling's last years were clouded by controversy. After the turn of the century he sold Hautbois Rectory to Frank Patteson, a retired Indian civil servant. It was a decision Girling lived to regret. Although, more than 40 years earlier, he had paid for the contruction of the house, it had been built on church land. He sold it without the permission of church authorities. A row with the diocese followed, and Girling was told to build a new rectory to replace the one he had sold. At considerable personal expense the former parsonage house in Rectory Road, Coltishall, was built. It was still under construction when he died.

In the wake of the rumpus Girling moved to Coltishall's old riverside rectory beside the Lower Common. There his health began to fail. He suffered a stroke of paralysis and, though his spirits periodically revived, he fell into a steady decline. On the evening of May 2nd, 1907, he had a game of cribbage with his son, Philip, then rector of Tunstead, before retiring to bed. After midnight he suffered fatal heart failure. His death was mourned by the whole community. The village school was closed on the day he was buried inside the ruins of old Hautbois Church - the church which, nearly 50 years earlier, he had made redundant. Philip Girling succeeded his father as rector of Coltishall and Great Hautbois between 1907-31. John Colk Girling's grand-daughter, Miss Dorothy Girling, who today lives in White Lion Road, can just remember sitting on her grandfather's knee as a young girl. She recalls being most upset when he died.

Once the centre of a diocesan controversy, Great Hautbois Rectory was built by the Rev. John Colk Girling shortly after his appointment to the parish in 1859. Picture by Brian Waite.

## SQUIRE OF ST.JAMES

Saturday August 20th, 1904, was a day of celebration for Robert Atkinson Gorell, probably the richest man ever to have lived at Coltishall.

More than 130 congratulatory telegrams and letters arrived at his home, the Old Hall, St.James. Flags were flown around the village in his honour. A special peal of bells rang out from the parish church during the afternoon and evening. All heralded his 100th birthday.

The grand old gentleman - Coltishall's first recorded centenarian - lived only a third of his long life at the Old Hall. Yet in that time he exercised a remarkable influence over the village, acting as magistrate, landowner, rector's churchwarden, parish guardian, school governor and wealthy benefactor. Among his many gifts to the village was the parish church clock, which greets the hour to this day. With Richard Rogers, of Coltishall Hall, and the Rev.John Colk Girling, the then rector, Gorell was one of a trio of formidable men who dominated Coltishall a century ago.

A clergyman's son, Gorell was born at Manserg Vicarage in Kirby Lonsdale, Westmoreland. After grammar school he started a business career at Liverpool at the tender age of 15, and in 1827 joined a Bradford firm of worsted spinners, John Rand and Sons. He moved to Norwich in 1841 to take charge of a branch of Rand's business at Duke Street, where he supplied cotton, silk and worsted yarn to the textile trade. Blessed with shrewd commercial judgement and boundless energy, Gorell prospered. In some 30 years as a city yarn merchant he became an archetypal Victorian self-made man, living in the genteel neighbourhood of Unthank Road, serving as a city councillor and magistrate and mixing in leading social circles.

Having made his fortune, Gorell retired from the textile trade in about 1870 and moved to Coltishall Old Hall. Elinor, his wife, died shortly afterwards, and for the rest of his life he lived with Sarah Jane, his only child. Top-hatted and distinguished, Gorell was quickly accepted into polite Coltishall society. A devout Anglican, he also formed a close friendship with the rector, John Girling.

Far from settling into a quiet, secluded retirement, Gorell embarked on what was probably the busiest period of his life. Prudent investment during his time in Norwich had made him a major shareholder in the Norwich Union Fire Insurance Society, and from the 1870s he took a leading role in its management. In 1877, aged 73, he was appointed to a powerful Norwich Union committee which radically reorganised the emerging insurance company. The shake-up laid the basis for unprecedented expansion, and during the last quarter of the century Gorell had the pleasure of watching the value of his shareholding soar. His reforming zeal was rewarded in 1880 with a seat on the Norwich Union board of directors, a position he was to hold until his 99th year.

Gorell was Coltishall's first commuter, travelling to Norwich daily after the opening of the branch railway line in 1879. His coachman, Henry Harmer, drove him to Coltishall station to catch the 9.30 a.m. train. There, Gorell insisted on the stationmaster, William Storey, having a roaring fire ready for him in the waiting room. In Norwich he attended the weekly meetings of the Norwich Union board. Minutes show he was a forceful director with an astute business mind. Aside from business he was on the board of the Norfolk and Norwich Hospital, and was made a member of its busy finance committee at the age of 86. He was a founder member of the Norwich Church of England Young Men's Society and a committee member of the Norwich Institution for the Blind.

At Coltishall, Gorell assumed the role of a benevolent country squire. He provided premises for Coltishall Cottage Hospital, later a nursing and

Self-made man - Robert Atkinson Gorell. (Courtesy Norwich CEYMS)

maternity home, which was a vital centre of health care between 1881-1959. At the parish church, where his attendance at services was unfailing, Gorell served as a churchwarden, sidesman and vestry committee member. In 1877 he paid £173 - equivalent to about 10 years' pay for a Victorian farm labourer - for the church tower clock, and in 1881 he made a gift of £100 for the building of the vestry. He belonged to the local Conservative Association, and with the help of his daughter established a thriving branch of the British and Foreign Bible Society in the village. He also developed a number of properties in the parish, including Jubilee Cottages in St. James.

As chairman of Coltishall Board School, Gorell wielded an autocratic authority over village education for nearly 20 years. He controlled virtually every aspect of school life, including the appointment of teaching staff, maintenance of discipline and declaration of school holidays. The schoolmaster, William Harper, was more than once at the receiving end of a sharp reprimand from the squire of St. James, who had his own ideas about how the school should run and its pupils behave. In the autumn of 1887, for example, Gorell made repeated complaints that the children of Coltishall did not bow and curtsy to the gentry of the village when they passed them in the streets. He ordered Harper to teach his pupils to be more respectful, and threatened to withdraw all school prizes for a year unless standards of politeness improved. After Gorell had issued his third broadside on street rudeness, the beleaguered Harper wrote: "The master said his authority did not extend into the streets, and that several parents had forbidden their children to obey this injunction ... The people here are on the whole very independent in opinion and demeanour, and the master feels that he is awkwardly placed in this matter of curtsying and bowing, since on the one hand the chairman (Gorell) insists upon it, and on the other the parents threaten their children with punishment if they curtsy and bow." Harper's remarks show how many working people in Coltishall resented the power and privileges of Gorell and his class, and were far removed from the cap-touching stereotype usually associated with country folk in the last century.

Gorell had a fascination for the inventions of the Victorian era. He was a frequent visitor to the 1851 Crystal Palace Great Exhibition, the famous showpiece of British industrial supremacy. His textile firm was among those awarded a medal at the exhibition. Gorell lived through the introduction of railways and the development of electricity, and kept informed of new innovations after his retirement by reading newspapers. The church clock he had installed at Coltishall was but one mechanical gadget to catch his eye.

Gorell's country seat - the Old Hall, St.James. Picture by Brian Waite.

Street lighting was another of his preoccupations. During the 1880s he distributed a large number of iron street lamps throughout the parish. Thanks to the gift, village streets were soon illuminated at night.

On entering his nineties, Gorell lost none of his appetite for life. He took pride in his age and vitality, and was fond of recounting events from the dim and distant past, including the Chartist riots of the 1830s, the Reform Bill controversy of 1832, the Crimean War and the Indian Mutiny campaign. In a letter to The Times in 1897, he recalled the jubilee of King George III in 1809, the Peninsular War - "a most exciting time" - and the surrender of Napoleon in 1814. He remembered attending the funeral of the Duke of Wellington at St. Paul's Cathedral in 1852 and witnessing the installation of the Prince Consort in 1847. "I am now in my 94th year of age; it is upwards of 142 years since the birth of my father, and I am thankful to say I am in full vigour of mind and body," he wrote. As if to prove his sprightly capabilities, Gorell travelled to London at the age of 93 to take part in celebrations to mark Queen Victoria's diamond jubilee. When he was 97 he tried to retire from the Norwich Union board on the grounds of his great age. His fellow directors would not let him. Declaring their unabated confidence in his business skills, they elected him for another term. When he eventually resigned in 1902 he was the oldest company director in Britain.

By the time of his 100th birthday Gorell was a local legend. Coltishall schoolchildren listened in awe to tales of the grand old man of the Old Hall who had lived in the reigns of five monarchs, from George III to Edward VII.

Gorell's gift to the village - now the Hermitage Rest Home, but established in 1881 as a cottage hospital. (Norfolk County Libraries)

Time waits for no man - especially Ben Jordan. He winds the parish church clock which was given to Coltishall in 1877 by Robert Atkinson Gorell. Picture by Brian Waite.

Villagers thought him immortal. On his birthday Gorell sat quietly in an easy chair in his bedroom as a team of Coltishall bellringers rang in his century. While celebrations took place in the village he received personal calls from well-wishers and read telegrams of congratulation from, among others, the Mayor of Norwich, the Norwich Union board, the CEYMS and the Norfolk and Norwich Hospital. At the Norwich Institute for the Blind, inmates were treated to a special high tea in his honour.

The end was nigh, however. In the run-up to his 100th birthday Gorell had to be nursed night and day as his health declined. After becoming a centenarian his condition rapidly deteriorated. On October 26th, 1904, with his daughter at his side, he died of senile decay. Coltishall mourned his passing as the end of an era. At his funeral at the parish church a large company of mourners, including the Mayor of Norwich, watched his coffin being lowered into a grand marble grave. The Dean of Norwich, delivering a funeral sermon, said: "He was no idler: as God gave him prosperity he did not relax his labours. He was an example that the busiest man might follow."

The bulk of Gorell's estate passed to Sarah Jane, his beloved daughter, who lived at the Old Hall until her death, aged 94, in 1931. She never married, and when her will was published later that year a family fortune of £226,588 - approximately £6 million in the currency of the 1980s - was revealed. Most of the money was inherited by Miss Isabel Ashenhurst, a niece of Sarah Jane's, who lived at Holly Lodge, Coltishall, until her death in 1965. Sarah Jane Gorell built St. Luke's Church, Catton, in memory of her father.

## THE VILLAGE TODAY

Since its Victorian heyday Coltishall has undergone a social revolution of considerable proportions. A century ago the village's overwhelmingly working-class population lived and worked locally, forming a closely-knit community existing on the margin of poverty. Ninety-five per cent of Coltishall people were of Norfolk birth and the village had a strong sense of identity, marking it off from surrounding parishes, especially the much-distrusted Horstead. A network of local families, including the Allens, Comans, Grouts, Harmers, Riseboroughs, Watts and Wrights, were the backbone of the community. Today many of those families remain, but since the Second World War the village has been transformed by an influx of affluent, predominantly middle-class newcomers. Relatively cheap housing has attracted scores of retired couples from the southern half of England, and the development of the nearby RAF station has brought a steady flow of servicemen's families. Numerous car-owning commuters have settled in the parish, and the number of holiday homes has also markedly increased in recent years.

The break-up of Coltishall's traditional rural economy of farming, malting and wherrybuilding, which took place earlier this century, was not followed by a regeneration of the local economy sufficient to provide jobs for a majority of village people. Commuting has therefore become the norm. Roys, the supermarket chain now based in Wroxham, ran a busy shop and bakery at Coltishall for many years, but both concerns were closed in the 1970s. Even the village's popularity with summer visitors and day trippers has failed to create job opportunities on a significant scale. Apart from a garage and a car dealer, several antiques shops, an insurance office, an estate agent, a craft centre, an electrical business, two rest homes, a post office, five public houses and a small number of shops supplying everyday needs, Coltishall is today but a shadow of its proud Victorian past.